# INCOME AND EXPENSE

## Log Book

NAME: ......................................................

ADDRESS: ................................................

PHONE: ....................................................

EMAIL: ......................................................

BOOK NO: .................................................

START DATE: .............................................

CONTINUED FROM BOOK NO: ....................

# INCOME & EXPENSE
## LOG BOOK

Year: 

Month: 

| Sr # | Date | Description | Income | Expenses | Balance |
|------|------|-------------|--------|----------|---------|
| | | | | | |
| | | | | | |
| | | | | | |
| | | | | | |
| | | | | | |
| | | | | | |
| | | | | | |
| | | | | | |
| | | | | | |
| | | | | | |
| | | | | | |
| | | | | | |
| | | | | | |
| | | | | | |
| | | | | | |
| | | | | | |
| | | | | | |
| | | | | | |
| | | | | | |
| | | **Total** | | | |

**NOTE**

# INCOME & EXPENSE
## LOG BOOK

**Year:** 

**Month:** 

| Sr # | Date | Description | Income | Expenses | Balance |
|------|------|-------------|--------|----------|---------|
| | | | | | |
| | | | | | |
| | | | | | |
| | | | | | |
| | | | | | |
| | | | | | |
| | | | | | |
| | | | | | |
| | | | | | |
| | | | | | |
| | | | | | |
| | | | | | |
| | | | | | |
| | | | | | |
| | | | | | |
| | | | | | |
| | | | | | |
| | | | | | |
| | | | | | |
| | | | | | |
| | **Total** | | | | |

**NOTE**

# INCOME & EXPENSE
## LOG BOOK

**Year:**

**Month:**

| Sr # | Date | Description | Income | Expenses | Balance |
|------|------|-------------|--------|----------|---------|
| | | | | | |
| | | | | | |
| | | | | | |
| | | | | | |
| | | | | | |
| | | | | | |
| | | | | | |
| | | | | | |
| | | | | | |
| | | | | | |
| | | | | | |
| | | | | | |
| | | | | | |
| | | | | | |
| | | | | | |
| | | | | | |
| | | | | | |
| | | | | | |
| | | | | | |
| | | **Total** | | | |

**NOTE**

# INCOME & EXPENSE
## LOG BOOK

**Year:**

**Month:**

| Sr # | Date | Description | Income | Expenses | Balance |
|---|---|---|---|---|---|
| | | | | | |
| | | | | | |
| | | | | | |
| | | | | | |
| | | | | | |
| | | | | | |
| | | | | | |
| | | | | | |
| | | | | | |
| | | | | | |
| | | | | | |
| | | | | | |
| | | | | | |
| | | | | | |
| | | | | | |
| | | | | | |
| | | | | | |
| | | | | | |
| | | | | | |
| | | | | | |
| | | | | | |
| | | **Total** | | | |

**NOTE**

# INCOME & EXPENSE
## LOG BOOK

Year:

Month:

| Sr # | Date | Description | Income | Expenses | Balance |
|------|------|-------------|--------|----------|---------|
| | | | | | |
| | | | | | |
| | | | | | |
| | | | | | |
| | | | | | |
| | | | | | |
| | | | | | |
| | | | | | |
| | | | | | |
| | | | | | |
| | | | | | |
| | | | | | |
| | | | | | |
| | | | | | |
| | | | | | |
| | | | | | |
| | | | | | |
| | | | | | |
| | | | | | |
| | | | | | |
| | **Total** | | | | |

**NOTE**

# INCOME & EXPENSE
## LOG BOOK

**Year:**

**Month:**

| Sr # | Date | Description | Income | Expenses | Balance |
|------|------|-------------|--------|----------|---------|
| | | | | | |
| | | | | | |
| | | | | | |
| | | | | | |
| | | | | | |
| | | | | | |
| | | | | | |
| | | | | | |
| | | | | | |
| | | | | | |
| | | | | | |
| | | | | | |
| | | | | | |
| | | | | | |
| | | | | | |
| | | | | | |
| | | | | | |
| | | | | | |
| | | | | | |
| | | | | | |
| | | **Total** | | | |

**NOTE**

# INCOME & EXPENSE
## LOG BOOK

Year:

Month:

| Sr # | Date | Description | Income | Expenses | Balance |
|------|------|-------------|--------|----------|---------|
|      |      |             |        |          |         |
|      |      |             |        |          |         |
|      |      |             |        |          |         |
|      |      |             |        |          |         |
|      |      |             |        |          |         |
|      |      |             |        |          |         |
|      |      |             |        |          |         |
|      |      |             |        |          |         |
|      |      |             |        |          |         |
|      |      |             |        |          |         |
|      |      |             |        |          |         |
|      |      |             |        |          |         |
|      |      |             |        |          |         |
|      |      |             |        |          |         |
|      |      |             |        |          |         |
|      |      |             |        |          |         |
|      |      |             |        |          |         |
|      |      |             |        |          |         |
|      |      |             |        |          |         |
|      |      | **Total**   |        |          |         |

**NOTE**

# INCOME & EXPENSE
## LOG BOOK

**Year:**

**Month:**

| Sr # | Date | Description | Income | Expenses | Balance |
|------|------|-------------|--------|----------|---------|
|      |      |             |        |          |         |
|      |      |             |        |          |         |
|      |      |             |        |          |         |
|      |      |             |        |          |         |
|      |      |             |        |          |         |
|      |      |             |        |          |         |
|      |      |             |        |          |         |
|      |      |             |        |          |         |
|      |      |             |        |          |         |
|      |      |             |        |          |         |
|      |      |             |        |          |         |
|      |      |             |        |          |         |
|      |      |             |        |          |         |
|      |      |             |        |          |         |
|      |      |             |        |          |         |
|      |      |             |        |          |         |
|      |      |             |        |          |         |
|      |      |             |        |          |         |
|      |      |             |        |          |         |
|      |      |             |        |          |         |
|      | **Total** |        |        |          |         |

**NOTE**

# INCOME & EXPENSE
## LOG BOOK

Year:

Month:

| Sr # | Date | Description | Income | Expenses | Balance |
|------|------|-------------|--------|----------|---------|
|  |  |  |  |  |  |
|  |  |  |  |  |  |
|  |  |  |  |  |  |
|  |  |  |  |  |  |
|  |  |  |  |  |  |
|  |  |  |  |  |  |
|  |  |  |  |  |  |
|  |  |  |  |  |  |
|  |  |  |  |  |  |
|  |  |  |  |  |  |
|  |  |  |  |  |  |
|  |  |  |  |  |  |
|  |  |  |  |  |  |
|  |  |  |  |  |  |
|  |  |  |  |  |  |
|  |  |  |  |  |  |
|  |  |  |  |  |  |
|  |  |  |  |  |  |
|  |  |  |  |  |  |
|  |  |  |  |  |  |
|  |  |  |  |  |  |
|  |  | **Total** |  |  |  |

**NOTE**

# INCOME & EXPENSE
## LOG BOOK

**Year:**

**Month:**

| Sr # | Date | Description | Income | Expenses | Balance |
|---|---|---|---|---|---|
| | | | | | |
| | | | | | |
| | | | | | |
| | | | | | |
| | | | | | |
| | | | | | |
| | | | | | |
| | | | | | |
| | | | | | |
| | | | | | |
| | | | | | |
| | | | | | |
| | | | | | |
| | | | | | |
| | | | | | |
| | | | | | |
| | | | | | |
| | | | | | |
| | | | | | |
| | **Total** | | | | |

**NOTE**

# INCOME & EXPENSE
## LOG BOOK

**Year:**

**Month:**

| Sr # | Date | Description | Income | Expenses | Balance |
|------|------|-------------|--------|----------|---------|
|      |      |             |        |          |         |
|      |      |             |        |          |         |
|      |      |             |        |          |         |
|      |      |             |        |          |         |
|      |      |             |        |          |         |
|      |      |             |        |          |         |
|      |      |             |        |          |         |
|      |      |             |        |          |         |
|      |      |             |        |          |         |
|      |      |             |        |          |         |
|      |      |             |        |          |         |
|      |      |             |        |          |         |
|      |      |             |        |          |         |
|      |      |             |        |          |         |
|      |      |             |        |          |         |
|      |      |             |        |          |         |
|      |      |             |        |          |         |
|      |      |             |        |          |         |
|      |      |             |        |          |         |
|      |      |             |        |          |         |
| **Total** | | | | | |

**NOTE**

# INCOME & EXPENSE
## LOG BOOK

Year:

Month:

| Sr # | Date | Description | Income | Expenses | Balance |
|------|------|-------------|--------|----------|---------|
|  |  |  |  |  |  |
|  |  |  |  |  |  |
|  |  |  |  |  |  |
|  |  |  |  |  |  |
|  |  |  |  |  |  |
|  |  |  |  |  |  |
|  |  |  |  |  |  |
|  |  |  |  |  |  |
|  |  |  |  |  |  |
|  |  |  |  |  |  |
|  |  |  |  |  |  |
|  |  |  |  |  |  |
|  |  |  |  |  |  |
|  |  |  |  |  |  |
|  |  |  |  |  |  |
|  |  |  |  |  |  |
|  |  |  |  |  |  |
|  |  |  |  |  |  |
|  |  |  |  |  |  |
|  |  |  |  |  |  |
|  |  | **Total** |  |  |  |

**NOTE**

# INCOME & EXPENSE
## LOG BOOK

**Year:**

**Month:**

| Sr # | Date | Description | Income | Expenses | Balance |
|------|------|-------------|--------|----------|---------|
| | | | | | |
| | | | | | |
| | | | | | |
| | | | | | |
| | | | | | |
| | | | | | |
| | | | | | |
| | | | | | |
| | | | | | |
| | | | | | |
| | | | | | |
| | | | | | |
| | | | | | |
| | | | | | |
| | | | | | |
| | | | | | |
| | | | | | |
| | | | | | |
| | | | | | |
| | | | | | |
| | | | | | |
| | | **Total** | | | |

**NOTE**

# INCOME & EXPENSE
## LOG BOOK

Year:

Month:

| Sr # | Date | Description | Income | Expenses | Balance |
|---|---|---|---|---|---|
| | | | | | |
| | | | | | |
| | | | | | |
| | | | | | |
| | | | | | |
| | | | | | |
| | | | | | |
| | | | | | |
| | | | | | |
| | | | | | |
| | | | | | |
| | | | | | |
| | | | | | |
| | | | | | |
| | | | | | |
| | | | | | |
| | | | | | |
| | | | | | |
| | | | | | |
| | | | | | |
| | | **Total** | | | |

**NOTE**

# INCOME & EXPENSE
## LOG BOOK

Year:

Month:

| Sr # | Date | Description | Income | Expenses | Balance |
|---|---|---|---|---|---|
| | | | | | |
| | | | | | |
| | | | | | |
| | | | | | |
| | | | | | |
| | | | | | |
| | | | | | |
| | | | | | |
| | | | | | |
| | | | | | |
| | | | | | |
| | | | | | |
| | | | | | |
| | | | | | |
| | | | | | |
| | | | | | |
| | | | | | |
| | | | | | |
| | | | | | |
| | | | | | |
| | | Total | | | |

**NOTE**

# INCOME & EXPENSE
## LOG BOOK

**Year:**

**Month:**

| Sr # | Date | Description | Income | Expenses | Balance |
|---|---|---|---|---|---|
| | | | | | |
| | | | | | |
| | | | | | |
| | | | | | |
| | | | | | |
| | | | | | |
| | | | | | |
| | | | | | |
| | | | | | |
| | | | | | |
| | | | | | |
| | | | | | |
| | | | | | |
| | | | | | |
| | | | | | |
| | | | | | |
| | | | | | |
| | | | | | |
| | | | | | |
| | | | | | |
| | | | | | |
| | | **Total** | | | |

**NOTE**

# INCOME & EXPENSE
## LOG BOOK

Year:

Month:

| Sr # | Date | Description | Income | Expenses | Balance |
|------|------|-------------|--------|----------|---------|
| | | | | | |
| | | | | | |
| | | | | | |
| | | | | | |
| | | | | | |
| | | | | | |
| | | | | | |
| | | | | | |
| | | | | | |
| | | | | | |
| | | | | | |
| | | | | | |
| | | | | | |
| | | | | | |
| | | | | | |
| | | | | | |
| | | | | | |
| | | | | | |
| | | | | | |
| | | | | | |
| | | Total | | | |

**NOTE**

# INCOME & EXPENSE
## LOG BOOK

**Year:**

**Month:**

| Sr # | Date | Description | Income | Expenses | Balance |
|------|------|-------------|--------|----------|---------|
| | | | | | |
| | | | | | |
| | | | | | |
| | | | | | |
| | | | | | |
| | | | | | |
| | | | | | |
| | | | | | |
| | | | | | |
| | | | | | |
| | | | | | |
| | | | | | |
| | | | | | |
| | | | | | |
| | | | | | |
| | | | | | |
| | | | | | |
| | | | | | |
| | | | | | |
| | | | | | |
| | | | | | |
| | | **Total** | | | |

**NOTE**

# INCOME & EXPENSE
## LOG BOOK

Year: 

Month: 

| Sr # | Date | Description | Income | Expenses | Balance |
|---|---|---|---|---|---|
| | | | | | |
| | | | | | |
| | | | | | |
| | | | | | |
| | | | | | |
| | | | | | |
| | | | | | |
| | | | | | |
| | | | | | |
| | | | | | |
| | | | | | |
| | | | | | |
| | | | | | |
| | | | | | |
| | | | | | |
| | | | | | |
| | | | | | |
| | | | | | |
| | | | | | |
| | | Total | | | |

**NOTE**

# INCOME & EXPENSE
## LOG BOOK

Year:

Month:

| Sr # | Date | Description | Income | Expenses | Balance |
|------|------|-------------|--------|----------|---------|
|  |  |  |  |  |  |
|  |  |  |  |  |  |
|  |  |  |  |  |  |
|  |  |  |  |  |  |
|  |  |  |  |  |  |
|  |  |  |  |  |  |
|  |  |  |  |  |  |
|  |  |  |  |  |  |
|  |  |  |  |  |  |
|  |  |  |  |  |  |
|  |  |  |  |  |  |
|  |  |  |  |  |  |
|  |  |  |  |  |  |
|  |  |  |  |  |  |
|  |  |  |  |  |  |
|  |  |  |  |  |  |
|  |  |  |  |  |  |
|  |  |  |  |  |  |
|  |  |  |  |  |  |
|  |  |  |  |  |  |
|  | **Total** |  |  |  |  |

**NOTE**

# INCOME & EXPENSE
## LOG BOOK

Year:

Month:

| Sr # | Date | Description | Income | Expenses | Balance |
|------|------|-------------|--------|----------|---------|
|      |      |             |        |          |         |
|      |      |             |        |          |         |
|      |      |             |        |          |         |
|      |      |             |        |          |         |
|      |      |             |        |          |         |
|      |      |             |        |          |         |
|      |      |             |        |          |         |
|      |      |             |        |          |         |
|      |      |             |        |          |         |
|      |      |             |        |          |         |
|      |      |             |        |          |         |
|      |      |             |        |          |         |
|      |      |             |        |          |         |
|      |      |             |        |          |         |
|      |      |             |        |          |         |
|      |      |             |        |          |         |
|      |      |             |        |          |         |
|      |      |             |        |          |         |
|      |      |             |        |          |         |
|      |      | Total       |        |          |         |

**NOTE**

# INCOME & EXPENSE
## LOG BOOK

**Year:**

**Month:**

| Sr # | Date | Description | Income | Expenses | Balance |
|------|------|-------------|--------|----------|---------|
| | | | | | |
| | | | | | |
| | | | | | |
| | | | | | |
| | | | | | |
| | | | | | |
| | | | | | |
| | | | | | |
| | | | | | |
| | | | | | |
| | | | | | |
| | | | | | |
| | | | | | |
| | | | | | |
| | | | | | |
| | | | | | |
| | | | | | |
| | | | | | |
| | | | | | |
| | | | | | |
| | | | | | |
| | **Total** | | | | |

**NOTE**

# INCOME & EXPENSE
## LOG BOOK

Year:

Month:

| Sr # | Date | Description | Income | Expenses | Balance |
|------|------|-------------|--------|----------|---------|
|  |  |  |  |  |  |
|  |  |  |  |  |  |
|  |  |  |  |  |  |
|  |  |  |  |  |  |
|  |  |  |  |  |  |
|  |  |  |  |  |  |
|  |  |  |  |  |  |
|  |  |  |  |  |  |
|  |  |  |  |  |  |
|  |  |  |  |  |  |
|  |  |  |  |  |  |
|  |  |  |  |  |  |
|  |  |  |  |  |  |
|  |  |  |  |  |  |
|  |  |  |  |  |  |
|  |  |  |  |  |  |
|  |  |  |  |  |  |
|  |  |  |  |  |  |
|  |  |  |  |  |  |
|  |  |  |  |  |  |
|  | | Total |  |  |  |

**NOTE**

# INCOME & EXPENSE
## LOG BOOK

Year: 

Month: 

| Sr # | Date | Description | Income | Expenses | Balance |
|---|---|---|---|---|---|
| | | | | | |
| | | | | | |
| | | | | | |
| | | | | | |
| | | | | | |
| | | | | | |
| | | | | | |
| | | | | | |
| | | | | | |
| | | | | | |
| | | | | | |
| | | | | | |
| | | | | | |
| | | | | | |
| | | | | | |
| | | | | | |
| | | | | | |
| | | | | | |
| | | | | | |
| | | | | | |
| | | | | | |
| | | | | | |
| | | Total | | | |

**NOTE**

# INCOME & EXPENSE
## LOG BOOK

Year: 
Month: 

| Sr # | Date | Description | Income | Expenses | Balance |
|------|------|-------------|--------|----------|---------|
|      |      |             |        |          |         |
|      |      |             |        |          |         |
|      |      |             |        |          |         |
|      |      |             |        |          |         |
|      |      |             |        |          |         |
|      |      |             |        |          |         |
|      |      |             |        |          |         |
|      |      |             |        |          |         |
|      |      |             |        |          |         |
|      |      |             |        |          |         |
|      |      |             |        |          |         |
|      |      |             |        |          |         |
|      |      |             |        |          |         |
|      |      |             |        |          |         |
|      |      |             |        |          |         |
|      |      |             |        |          |         |
|      |      |             |        |          |         |
|      |      |             |        |          |         |
|      |      |             |        |          |         |
|      |      |             |        |          |         |
|      |      | Total       |        |          |         |

**NOTE**

# INCOME & EXPENSE
## LOG BOOK

**Year:**

**Month:**

| Sr # | Date | Description | Income | Expenses | Balance |
|------|------|-------------|--------|----------|---------|
| | | | | | |
| | | | | | |
| | | | | | |
| | | | | | |
| | | | | | |
| | | | | | |
| | | | | | |
| | | | | | |
| | | | | | |
| | | | | | |
| | | | | | |
| | | | | | |
| | | | | | |
| | | | | | |
| | | | | | |
| | | | | | |
| | | | | | |
| | | | | | |
| | | | | | |
| | | | | | |
| | | **Total** | | | |

**NOTE**

# INCOME & EXPENSE
## LOG BOOK

Year:

Month:

| Sr # | Date | Description | Income | Expenses | Balance |
|------|------|-------------|--------|----------|---------|
|  |  |  |  |  |  |
|  |  |  |  |  |  |
|  |  |  |  |  |  |
|  |  |  |  |  |  |
|  |  |  |  |  |  |
|  |  |  |  |  |  |
|  |  |  |  |  |  |
|  |  |  |  |  |  |
|  |  |  |  |  |  |
|  |  |  |  |  |  |
|  |  |  |  |  |  |
|  |  |  |  |  |  |
|  |  |  |  |  |  |
|  |  |  |  |  |  |
|  |  |  |  |  |  |
|  |  |  |  |  |  |
|  |  |  |  |  |  |
|  |  |  |  |  |  |
|  |  |  |  |  |  |
|  |  |  |  |  |  |
|  |  |  |  |  |  |
|  |  | **Total** |  |  |  |

**NOTE**

# INCOME & EXPENSE
## LOG BOOK

Year:

Month:

| Sr # | Date | Description | Income | Expenses | Balance |
|---|---|---|---|---|---|
| | | | | | |
| | | | | | |
| | | | | | |
| | | | | | |
| | | | | | |
| | | | | | |
| | | | | | |
| | | | | | |
| | | | | | |
| | | | | | |
| | | | | | |
| | | | | | |
| | | | | | |
| | | | | | |
| | | | | | |
| | | | | | |
| | | | | | |
| | | | | | |
| | | | | | |
| | | Total | | | |

**NOTE**

# INCOME & EXPENSE
## LOG BOOK

Year:

Month:

| Sr # | Date | Description | Income | Expenses | Balance |
|------|------|-------------|--------|----------|---------|
|      |      |             |        |          |         |
|      |      |             |        |          |         |
|      |      |             |        |          |         |
|      |      |             |        |          |         |
|      |      |             |        |          |         |
|      |      |             |        |          |         |
|      |      |             |        |          |         |
|      |      |             |        |          |         |
|      |      |             |        |          |         |
|      |      |             |        |          |         |
|      |      |             |        |          |         |
|      |      |             |        |          |         |
|      |      |             |        |          |         |
|      |      |             |        |          |         |
|      |      |             |        |          |         |
|      |      |             |        |          |         |
|      |      |             |        |          |         |
|      |      |             |        |          |         |
|      |      |             |        |          |         |
|      | Total |            |        |          |         |

**NOTE**

# INCOME & EXPENSE
## LOG BOOK

Year:

Month:

| Sr # | Date | Description | Income | Expenses | Balance |
|------|------|-------------|--------|----------|---------|
| | | | | | |
| | | | | | |
| | | | | | |
| | | | | | |
| | | | | | |
| | | | | | |
| | | | | | |
| | | | | | |
| | | | | | |
| | | | | | |
| | | | | | |
| | | | | | |
| | | | | | |
| | | | | | |
| | | | | | |
| | | | | | |
| | | | | | |
| | | | | | |
| | | | | | |
| | | | | | |
| | | | | | |
| | | | | | |
| | | | | | |
| | | Total | | | |

**NOTE**

# INCOME & EXPENSE
## LOG BOOK

Year: 

Month: 

| Sr # | Date | Description | Income | Expenses | Balance |
|------|------|-------------|--------|----------|---------|
|  |  |  |  |  |  |
|  |  |  |  |  |  |
|  |  |  |  |  |  |
|  |  |  |  |  |  |
|  |  |  |  |  |  |
|  |  |  |  |  |  |
|  |  |  |  |  |  |
|  |  |  |  |  |  |
|  |  |  |  |  |  |
|  |  |  |  |  |  |
|  |  |  |  |  |  |
|  |  |  |  |  |  |
|  |  |  |  |  |  |
|  |  |  |  |  |  |
|  |  |  |  |  |  |
|  |  |  |  |  |  |
|  |  |  |  |  |  |
|  |  |  |  |  |  |
|  |  |  |  |  |  |
|  |  |  |  |  |  |
|  | | **Total** |  |  |  |

**NOTE**

# INCOME & EXPENSE
## LOG BOOK

Year: 
Month: 

| Sr # | Date | Description | Income | Expenses | Balance |
|------|------|-------------|--------|----------|---------|
| | | | | | |
| | | | | | |
| | | | | | |
| | | | | | |
| | | | | | |
| | | | | | |
| | | | | | |
| | | | | | |
| | | | | | |
| | | | | | |
| | | | | | |
| | | | | | |
| | | | | | |
| | | | | | |
| | | | | | |
| | | | | | |
| | | | | | |
| | | | | | |
| | | | | | |
| | | | | | |
| | | Total | | | |

**NOTE**

# INCOME & EXPENSE
## LOG BOOK

Year:

Month:

| Sr # | Date | Description | Income | Expenses | Balance |
|------|------|-------------|--------|----------|---------|
| | | | | | |
| | | | | | |
| | | | | | |
| | | | | | |
| | | | | | |
| | | | | | |
| | | | | | |
| | | | | | |
| | | | | | |
| | | | | | |
| | | | | | |
| | | | | | |
| | | | | | |
| | | | | | |
| | | | | | |
| | | | | | |
| | | | | | |
| | | | | | |
| | | | | | |
| | | | | | |
| | | Total | | | |

**NOTE**

# INCOME & EXPENSE
## LOG BOOK

Year:

Month:

| Sr # | Date | Description | Income | Expenses | Balance |
|------|------|-------------|--------|----------|---------|
|  |  |  |  |  |  |
|  |  |  |  |  |  |
|  |  |  |  |  |  |
|  |  |  |  |  |  |
|  |  |  |  |  |  |
|  |  |  |  |  |  |
|  |  |  |  |  |  |
|  |  |  |  |  |  |
|  |  |  |  |  |  |
|  |  |  |  |  |  |
|  |  |  |  |  |  |
|  |  |  |  |  |  |
|  |  |  |  |  |  |
|  |  |  |  |  |  |
|  |  |  |  |  |  |
|  |  |  |  |  |  |
|  |  |  |  |  |  |
|  |  |  |  |  |  |
|  |  |  |  |  |  |
|  |  |  |  |  |  |
|  |  |  |  |  |  |
|  |  | **Total** |  |  |  |

**NOTE**

# INCOME & EXPENSE
## LOG BOOK

**Year:**

**Month:**

| Sr # | Date | Description | Income | Expenses | Balance |
|------|------|-------------|--------|----------|---------|
| | | | | | |
| | | | | | |
| | | | | | |
| | | | | | |
| | | | | | |
| | | | | | |
| | | | | | |
| | | | | | |
| | | | | | |
| | | | | | |
| | | | | | |
| | | | | | |
| | | | | | |
| | | | | | |
| | | | | | |
| | | | | | |
| | | | | | |
| | | | | | |
| | | | | | |
| | | | | | |
| | | | | | |
| | Total | | | | |

**NOTE**

# INCOME & EXPENSE
## LOG BOOK

Year:

Month:

| Sr # | Date | Description | Income | Expenses | Balance |
|------|------|-------------|--------|----------|---------|
|      |      |             |        |          |         |
|      |      |             |        |          |         |
|      |      |             |        |          |         |
|      |      |             |        |          |         |
|      |      |             |        |          |         |
|      |      |             |        |          |         |
|      |      |             |        |          |         |
|      |      |             |        |          |         |
|      |      |             |        |          |         |
|      |      |             |        |          |         |
|      |      |             |        |          |         |
|      |      |             |        |          |         |
|      |      |             |        |          |         |
|      |      |             |        |          |         |
|      |      |             |        |          |         |
|      |      |             |        |          |         |
|      |      |             |        |          |         |
|      |      |             |        |          |         |
|      |      |             |        |          |         |
|      |      |             |        |          |         |
|      |      |             |        |          |         |
|      |      | **Total**   |        |          |         |

**NOTE**

# INCOME & EXPENSE
## LOG BOOK

Year:

Month:

| Sr # | Date | Description | Income | Expenses | Balance |
|------|------|-------------|--------|----------|---------|
|      |      |             |        |          |         |
|      |      |             |        |          |         |
|      |      |             |        |          |         |
|      |      |             |        |          |         |
|      |      |             |        |          |         |
|      |      |             |        |          |         |
|      |      |             |        |          |         |
|      |      |             |        |          |         |
|      |      |             |        |          |         |
|      |      |             |        |          |         |
|      |      |             |        |          |         |
|      |      |             |        |          |         |
|      |      |             |        |          |         |
|      |      |             |        |          |         |
|      |      |             |        |          |         |
|      |      |             |        |          |         |
|      |      |             |        |          |         |
|      |      |             |        |          |         |
|      |      |             |        |          |         |
|      |      | **Total**   |        |          |         |

**NOTE**

# INCOME & EXPENSE
## LOG BOOK

Year: 

Month: 

| Sr # | Date | Description | Income | Expenses | Balance |
|------|------|-------------|--------|----------|---------|
| | | | | | |
| | | | | | |
| | | | | | |
| | | | | | |
| | | | | | |
| | | | | | |
| | | | | | |
| | | | | | |
| | | | | | |
| | | | | | |
| | | | | | |
| | | | | | |
| | | | | | |
| | | | | | |
| | | | | | |
| | | | | | |
| | | | | | |
| | | | | | |
| | | | | | |
| | | | | | |
| | | | | | |
| | | | | | |
| | | | | | |
| | Total | | | | |

**NOTE**

# INCOME & EXPENSE
## LOG BOOK

Year:

Month:

| Sr # | Date | Description | Income | Expenses | Balance |
|---|---|---|---|---|---|
| | | | | | |
| | | | | | |
| | | | | | |
| | | | | | |
| | | | | | |
| | | | | | |
| | | | | | |
| | | | | | |
| | | | | | |
| | | | | | |
| | | | | | |
| | | | | | |
| | | | | | |
| | | | | | |
| | | | | | |
| | | | | | |
| | | | | | |
| | | | | | |
| | | | | | |
| | | | | | |
| | Total | | | | |

**NOTE**

# INCOME & EXPENSE
## LOG BOOK

Year:

Month:

| Sr # | Date | Description | Income | Expenses | Balance |
|---|---|---|---|---|---|
| | | | | | |
| | | | | | |
| | | | | | |
| | | | | | |
| | | | | | |
| | | | | | |
| | | | | | |
| | | | | | |
| | | | | | |
| | | | | | |
| | | | | | |
| | | | | | |
| | | | | | |
| | | | | | |
| | | | | | |
| | | | | | |
| | | | | | |
| | | | | | |
| | | | | | |
| | | | | | |
| | Total | | | | |

**NOTE**

# INCOME & EXPENSE
## LOG BOOK

Year: 

Month: 

| Sr # | Date | Description | Income | Expenses | Balance |
|------|------|-------------|--------|----------|---------|
|      |      |             |        |          |         |
|      |      |             |        |          |         |
|      |      |             |        |          |         |
|      |      |             |        |          |         |
|      |      |             |        |          |         |
|      |      |             |        |          |         |
|      |      |             |        |          |         |
|      |      |             |        |          |         |
|      |      |             |        |          |         |
|      |      |             |        |          |         |
|      |      |             |        |          |         |
|      |      |             |        |          |         |
|      |      |             |        |          |         |
|      |      |             |        |          |         |
|      |      |             |        |          |         |
|      |      |             |        |          |         |
|      |      |             |        |          |         |
|      |      |             |        |          |         |
|      |      |             |        |          |         |
|      |      | **Total**   |        |          |         |

**NOTE**

# INCOME & EXPENSE
## LOG BOOK

Year:

Month:

| Sr # | Date | Description | Income | Expenses | Balance |
|------|------|-------------|--------|----------|---------|
|      |      |             |        |          |         |
|      |      |             |        |          |         |
|      |      |             |        |          |         |
|      |      |             |        |          |         |
|      |      |             |        |          |         |
|      |      |             |        |          |         |
|      |      |             |        |          |         |
|      |      |             |        |          |         |
|      |      |             |        |          |         |
|      |      |             |        |          |         |
|      |      |             |        |          |         |
|      |      |             |        |          |         |
|      |      |             |        |          |         |
|      |      |             |        |          |         |
|      |      |             |        |          |         |
|      |      |             |        |          |         |
|      |      |             |        |          |         |
|      |      |             |        |          |         |
|      |      |             |        |          |         |
|      | **Total** |        |        |          |         |

**NOTE**

# INCOME & EXPENSE
## LOG BOOK

**Year:**

**Month:**

| Sr # | Date | Description | Income | Expenses | Balance |
|------|------|-------------|--------|----------|---------|
| | | | | | |
| | | | | | |
| | | | | | |
| | | | | | |
| | | | | | |
| | | | | | |
| | | | | | |
| | | | | | |
| | | | | | |
| | | | | | |
| | | | | | |
| | | | | | |
| | | | | | |
| | | | | | |
| | | | | | |
| | | | | | |
| | | | | | |
| | | | | | |
| | | | | | |
| | | | | | |
| | | **Total** | | | |

**NOTE**

# INCOME & EXPENSE
## LOG BOOK

**Year:**

**Month:**

| Sr # | Date | Description | Income | Expenses | Balance |
|------|------|-------------|--------|----------|---------|
|      |      |             |        |          |         |
|      |      |             |        |          |         |
|      |      |             |        |          |         |
|      |      |             |        |          |         |
|      |      |             |        |          |         |
|      |      |             |        |          |         |
|      |      |             |        |          |         |
|      |      |             |        |          |         |
|      |      |             |        |          |         |
|      |      |             |        |          |         |
|      |      |             |        |          |         |
|      |      |             |        |          |         |
|      |      |             |        |          |         |
|      |      |             |        |          |         |
|      |      |             |        |          |         |
|      |      |             |        |          |         |
|      |      |             |        |          |         |
|      |      |             |        |          |         |
|      |      |             |        |          |         |
|      |      |             |        |          |         |
| **Total** | | | | | |

**NOTE**

# INCOME & EXPENSE
## LOG BOOK

**Year:**

**Month:**

| Sr # | Date | Description | Income | Expenses | Balance |
|------|------|-------------|--------|----------|---------|
|      |      |             |        |          |         |
|      |      |             |        |          |         |
|      |      |             |        |          |         |
|      |      |             |        |          |         |
|      |      |             |        |          |         |
|      |      |             |        |          |         |
|      |      |             |        |          |         |
|      |      |             |        |          |         |
|      |      |             |        |          |         |
|      |      |             |        |          |         |
|      |      |             |        |          |         |
|      |      |             |        |          |         |
|      |      |             |        |          |         |
|      |      |             |        |          |         |
|      |      |             |        |          |         |
|      |      |             |        |          |         |
|      |      |             |        |          |         |
|      |      |             |        |          |         |
|      |      |             |        |          |         |
|      |      |             |        |          |         |
|      |      |             |        |          |         |
|      |      | **Total**   |        |          |         |

**NOTE**

# INCOME & EXPENSE
## LOG BOOK

Year:

Month:

| Sr # | Date | Description | Income | Expenses | Balance |
|---|---|---|---|---|---|
| | | | | | |
| | | | | | |
| | | | | | |
| | | | | | |
| | | | | | |
| | | | | | |
| | | | | | |
| | | | | | |
| | | | | | |
| | | | | | |
| | | | | | |
| | | | | | |
| | | | | | |
| | | | | | |
| | | | | | |
| | | | | | |
| | | | | | |
| | | | | | |
| | | | | | |
| | | | | | |
| | | | | | |
| | | | | | |
| | | **Total** | | | |

**NOTE**

# INCOME & EXPENSE
## LOG BOOK

Year: _____

Month: _____

| Sr # | Date | Description | Income | Expenses | Balance |
|------|------|-------------|--------|----------|---------|
|      |      |             |        |          |         |
|      |      |             |        |          |         |
|      |      |             |        |          |         |
|      |      |             |        |          |         |
|      |      |             |        |          |         |
|      |      |             |        |          |         |
|      |      |             |        |          |         |
|      |      |             |        |          |         |
|      |      |             |        |          |         |
|      |      |             |        |          |         |
|      |      |             |        |          |         |
|      |      |             |        |          |         |
|      |      |             |        |          |         |
|      |      |             |        |          |         |
|      |      |             |        |          |         |
|      |      |             |        |          |         |
|      |      |             |        |          |         |
|      |      |             |        |          |         |
|      |      |             |        |          |         |
|      |      |             |        |          |         |
|      |      | **Total**   |        |          |         |

**NOTE** _____

# INCOME & EXPENSE
## LOG BOOK

**Year:**

**Month:**

| Sr # | Date | Description | Income | Expenses | Balance |
|------|------|-------------|--------|----------|---------|
|  |  |  |  |  |  |
|  |  |  |  |  |  |
|  |  |  |  |  |  |
|  |  |  |  |  |  |
|  |  |  |  |  |  |
|  |  |  |  |  |  |
|  |  |  |  |  |  |
|  |  |  |  |  |  |
|  |  |  |  |  |  |
|  |  |  |  |  |  |
|  |  |  |  |  |  |
|  |  |  |  |  |  |
|  |  |  |  |  |  |
|  |  |  |  |  |  |
|  |  |  |  |  |  |
|  |  |  |  |  |  |
|  |  |  |  |  |  |
|  |  |  |  |  |  |
|  |  |  |  |  |  |
|  | **Total** |  |  |  |  |

**NOTE**

# INCOME & EXPENSE
## LOG BOOK

Year: 
Month: 

| Sr # | Date | Description | Income | Expenses | Balance |
|---|---|---|---|---|---|
| | | | | | |
| | | | | | |
| | | | | | |
| | | | | | |
| | | | | | |
| | | | | | |
| | | | | | |
| | | | | | |
| | | | | | |
| | | | | | |
| | | | | | |
| | | | | | |
| | | | | | |
| | | | | | |
| | | | | | |
| | | | | | |
| | | | | | |
| | | | | | |
| | | | | | |
| | | | | | |
| | | | | | |
| | | Total | | | |

**NOTE**

# INCOME & EXPENSE
## LOG BOOK

**Year:**

**Month:**

| Sr # | Date | Description | Income | Expenses | Balance |
|------|------|-------------|--------|----------|---------|
| | | | | | |
| | | | | | |
| | | | | | |
| | | | | | |
| | | | | | |
| | | | | | |
| | | | | | |
| | | | | | |
| | | | | | |
| | | | | | |
| | | | | | |
| | | | | | |
| | | | | | |
| | | | | | |
| | | | | | |
| | | | | | |
| | | | | | |
| | | | | | |
| | | | | | |
| | | | | | |
| | | | | | |
| | | | | | |
| | | **Total** | | | |

**NOTE**

# INCOME & EXPENSE
## LOG BOOK

Year:

Month:

| Sr # | Date | Description | Income | Expenses | Balance |
|------|------|-------------|--------|----------|---------|
| | | | | | |
| | | | | | |
| | | | | | |
| | | | | | |
| | | | | | |
| | | | | | |
| | | | | | |
| | | | | | |
| | | | | | |
| | | | | | |
| | | | | | |
| | | | | | |
| | | | | | |
| | | | | | |
| | | | | | |
| | | | | | |
| | | | | | |
| | | | | | |
| | | | | | |
| | Total | | | | |

**NOTE**

# INCOME & EXPENSE
## LOG BOOK

**Year:**

**Month:**

| Sr # | Date | Description | Income | Expenses | Balance |
|------|------|-------------|--------|----------|---------|
|  |  |  |  |  |  |
|  |  |  |  |  |  |
|  |  |  |  |  |  |
|  |  |  |  |  |  |
|  |  |  |  |  |  |
|  |  |  |  |  |  |
|  |  |  |  |  |  |
|  |  |  |  |  |  |
|  |  |  |  |  |  |
|  |  |  |  |  |  |
|  |  |  |  |  |  |
|  |  |  |  |  |  |
|  |  |  |  |  |  |
|  |  |  |  |  |  |
|  |  |  |  |  |  |
|  |  |  |  |  |  |
|  |  |  |  |  |  |
|  |  |  |  |  |  |
|  |  |  |  |  |  |
|  |  |  |  |  |  |
|  | | **Total** |  |  |  |

**NOTE**

# INCOME & EXPENSE
## LOG BOOK

Year:

Month:

| Sr # | Date | Description | Income | Expenses | Balance |
|------|------|-------------|--------|----------|---------|
|  |  |  |  |  |  |
|  |  |  |  |  |  |
|  |  |  |  |  |  |
|  |  |  |  |  |  |
|  |  |  |  |  |  |
|  |  |  |  |  |  |
|  |  |  |  |  |  |
|  |  |  |  |  |  |
|  |  |  |  |  |  |
|  |  |  |  |  |  |
|  |  |  |  |  |  |
|  |  |  |  |  |  |
|  |  |  |  |  |  |
|  |  |  |  |  |  |
|  |  |  |  |  |  |
|  |  |  |  |  |  |
|  |  |  |  |  |  |
|  |  |  |  |  |  |
|  |  |  |  |  |  |
|  |  |  |  |  |  |
|  |  | **Total** |  |  |  |

**NOTE**

# INCOME & EXPENSE
## LOG BOOK

Year:

Month:

| Sr # | Date | Description | Income | Expenses | Balance |
|------|------|-------------|--------|----------|---------|
|  |  |  |  |  |  |
|  |  |  |  |  |  |
|  |  |  |  |  |  |
|  |  |  |  |  |  |
|  |  |  |  |  |  |
|  |  |  |  |  |  |
|  |  |  |  |  |  |
|  |  |  |  |  |  |
|  |  |  |  |  |  |
|  |  |  |  |  |  |
|  |  |  |  |  |  |
|  |  |  |  |  |  |
|  |  |  |  |  |  |
|  |  |  |  |  |  |
|  |  |  |  |  |  |
|  |  |  |  |  |  |
|  |  |  |  |  |  |
|  |  |  |  |  |  |
|  |  |  |  |  |  |
| Total |  |  |  |  |  |

**NOTE**

# INCOME & EXPENSE
## LOG BOOK

**Year:**

**Month:**

| Sr # | Date | Description | Income | Expenses | Balance |
|---|---|---|---|---|---|
| | | | | | |
| | | | | | |
| | | | | | |
| | | | | | |
| | | | | | |
| | | | | | |
| | | | | | |
| | | | | | |
| | | | | | |
| | | | | | |
| | | | | | |
| | | | | | |
| | | | | | |
| | | | | | |
| | | | | | |
| | | | | | |
| | | | | | |
| | | | | | |
| | | | | | |
| | Total | | | | |

**NOTE**

# INCOME & EXPENSE
## LOG BOOK

**Year:**

**Month:**

| Sr # | Date | Description | Income | Expenses | Balance |
|---|---|---|---|---|---|
| | | | | | |
| | | | | | |
| | | | | | |
| | | | | | |
| | | | | | |
| | | | | | |
| | | | | | |
| | | | | | |
| | | | | | |
| | | | | | |
| | | | | | |
| | | | | | |
| | | | | | |
| | | | | | |
| | | | | | |
| | | | | | |
| | | | | | |
| | | | | | |
| | | | | | |
| | | | | | |
| | | | | | |
| | | | | | |
| | | **Total** | | | |

**NOTE**

# INCOME & EXPENSE
## LOG BOOK

**Year:**

**Month:**

| Sr # | Date | Description | Income | Expenses | Balance |
|------|------|-------------|--------|----------|---------|
|      |      |             |        |          |         |
|      |      |             |        |          |         |
|      |      |             |        |          |         |
|      |      |             |        |          |         |
|      |      |             |        |          |         |
|      |      |             |        |          |         |
|      |      |             |        |          |         |
|      |      |             |        |          |         |
|      |      |             |        |          |         |
|      |      |             |        |          |         |
|      |      |             |        |          |         |
|      |      |             |        |          |         |
|      |      |             |        |          |         |
|      |      |             |        |          |         |
|      |      |             |        |          |         |
|      |      |             |        |          |         |
|      |      |             |        |          |         |
|      |      |             |        |          |         |
|      |      |             |        |          |         |
|      |      |             |        |          |         |
| **Total** | | | | | |

**NOTE**

# INCOME & EXPENSE
## LOG BOOK

**Year:**

**Month:**

| Sr # | Date | Description | Income | Expenses | Balance |
|------|------|-------------|--------|----------|---------|
|      |      |             |        |          |         |
|      |      |             |        |          |         |
|      |      |             |        |          |         |
|      |      |             |        |          |         |
|      |      |             |        |          |         |
|      |      |             |        |          |         |
|      |      |             |        |          |         |
|      |      |             |        |          |         |
|      |      |             |        |          |         |
|      |      |             |        |          |         |
|      |      |             |        |          |         |
|      |      |             |        |          |         |
|      |      |             |        |          |         |
|      |      |             |        |          |         |
|      |      |             |        |          |         |
|      |      |             |        |          |         |
|      |      |             |        |          |         |
|      |      |             |        |          |         |
|      |      |             |        |          |         |
|      |      |             |        |          |         |
|      |      | **Total**   |        |          |         |

**NOTE**

# INCOME & EXPENSE
## LOG BOOK

**Year:**

**Month:**

| Sr # | Date | Description | Income | Expenses | Balance |
|---|---|---|---|---|---|
| | | | | | |
| | | | | | |
| | | | | | |
| | | | | | |
| | | | | | |
| | | | | | |
| | | | | | |
| | | | | | |
| | | | | | |
| | | | | | |
| | | | | | |
| | | | | | |
| | | | | | |
| | | | | | |
| | | | | | |
| | | | | | |
| | | | | | |
| | | | | | |
| | | | | | |
| | **Total** | | | | |

**NOTE**

# INCOME & EXPENSE
## LOG BOOK

Year: _____

Month: _____

| Sr # | Date | Description | Income | Expenses | Balance |
|------|------|-------------|--------|----------|---------|
| | | | | | |
| | | | | | |
| | | | | | |
| | | | | | |
| | | | | | |
| | | | | | |
| | | | | | |
| | | | | | |
| | | | | | |
| | | | | | |
| | | | | | |
| | | | | | |
| | | | | | |
| | | | | | |
| | | | | | |
| | | | | | |
| | | | | | |
| | | | | | |
| | | | | | |
| | Total | | | | |

**NOTE**

# INCOME & EXPENSE
## LOG BOOK

Year:

Month:

| Sr # | Date | Description | Income | Expenses | Balance |
|------|------|-------------|--------|----------|---------|
|      |      |             |        |          |         |
|      |      |             |        |          |         |
|      |      |             |        |          |         |
|      |      |             |        |          |         |
|      |      |             |        |          |         |
|      |      |             |        |          |         |
|      |      |             |        |          |         |
|      |      |             |        |          |         |
|      |      |             |        |          |         |
|      |      |             |        |          |         |
|      |      |             |        |          |         |
|      |      |             |        |          |         |
|      |      |             |        |          |         |
|      |      |             |        |          |         |
|      |      |             |        |          |         |
|      |      |             |        |          |         |
|      |      |             |        |          |         |
|      |      |             |        |          |         |
|      |      |             |        |          |         |
|      |      |             |        |          |         |
| | | **Total** | | | |

**NOTE**

# INCOME & EXPENSE
## LOG BOOK

**Year:**

**Month:**

| Sr # | Date | Description | Income | Expenses | Balance |
|------|------|-------------|--------|----------|---------|
|      |      |             |        |          |         |
|      |      |             |        |          |         |
|      |      |             |        |          |         |
|      |      |             |        |          |         |
|      |      |             |        |          |         |
|      |      |             |        |          |         |
|      |      |             |        |          |         |
|      |      |             |        |          |         |
|      |      |             |        |          |         |
|      |      |             |        |          |         |
|      |      |             |        |          |         |
|      |      |             |        |          |         |
|      |      |             |        |          |         |
|      |      |             |        |          |         |
|      |      |             |        |          |         |
|      |      |             |        |          |         |
|      |      |             |        |          |         |
|      |      |             |        |          |         |
|      |      |             |        |          |         |
|      |      |             |        |          |         |
|      |      |             |        |          |         |
|      |      | **Total**   |        |          |         |

**NOTE**

# INCOME & EXPENSE
## LOG BOOK

**Year:**

**Month:**

| Sr # | Date | Description | Income | Expenses | Balance |
|---|---|---|---|---|---|
| | | | | | |
| | | | | | |
| | | | | | |
| | | | | | |
| | | | | | |
| | | | | | |
| | | | | | |
| | | | | | |
| | | | | | |
| | | | | | |
| | | | | | |
| | | | | | |
| | | | | | |
| | | | | | |
| | | | | | |
| | | | | | |
| | | | | | |
| | | | | | |
| | | | | | |
| | | **Total** | | | |

**NOTE**

# INCOME & EXPENSE
## LOG BOOK

Year: 

Month: 

| Sr # | Date | Description | Income | Expenses | Balance |
|------|------|-------------|--------|----------|---------|
|      |      |             |        |          |         |
|      |      |             |        |          |         |
|      |      |             |        |          |         |
|      |      |             |        |          |         |
|      |      |             |        |          |         |
|      |      |             |        |          |         |
|      |      |             |        |          |         |
|      |      |             |        |          |         |
|      |      |             |        |          |         |
|      |      |             |        |          |         |
|      |      |             |        |          |         |
|      |      |             |        |          |         |
|      |      |             |        |          |         |
|      |      |             |        |          |         |
|      |      |             |        |          |         |
|      |      |             |        |          |         |
|      |      |             |        |          |         |
|      |      |             |        |          |         |
|      |      |             |        |          |         |
|      |      | **Total**   |        |          |         |

**NOTE**

# INCOME & EXPENSE
## LOG BOOK

Year: 

Month: 

| Sr # | Date | Description | Income | Expenses | Balance |
|------|------|-------------|--------|----------|---------|
| | | | | | |
| | | | | | |
| | | | | | |
| | | | | | |
| | | | | | |
| | | | | | |
| | | | | | |
| | | | | | |
| | | | | | |
| | | | | | |
| | | | | | |
| | | | | | |
| | | | | | |
| | | | | | |
| | | | | | |
| | | | | | |
| | | | | | |
| | | | | | |
| | | Total | | | |

**NOTE**

# INCOME & EXPENSE
## LOG BOOK

**Year:**

**Month:**

| Sr # | Date | Description | Income | Expenses | Balance |
|---|---|---|---|---|---|
| | | | | | |
| | | | | | |
| | | | | | |
| | | | | | |
| | | | | | |
| | | | | | |
| | | | | | |
| | | | | | |
| | | | | | |
| | | | | | |
| | | | | | |
| | | | | | |
| | | | | | |
| | | | | | |
| | | | | | |
| | | | | | |
| | | | | | |
| | | | | | |
| | | | | | |
| | | | | | |
| | | **Total** | | | |

**NOTE**

# INCOME & EXPENSE
## LOG BOOK

Year: 

Month: 

| Sr # | Date | Description | Income | Expenses | Balance |
|------|------|-------------|--------|----------|---------|
| | | | | | |
| | | | | | |
| | | | | | |
| | | | | | |
| | | | | | |
| | | | | | |
| | | | | | |
| | | | | | |
| | | | | | |
| | | | | | |
| | | | | | |
| | | | | | |
| | | | | | |
| | | | | | |
| | | | | | |
| | | | | | |
| | | | | | |
| | | | | | |
| | | | | | |
| | | | | | |
| | | Total | | | |

**NOTE**

# INCOME & EXPENSE
## LOG BOOK

Year: 

Month: 

| Sr # | Date | Description | Income | Expenses | Balance |
|------|------|-------------|--------|----------|---------|
|      |      |             |        |          |         |
|      |      |             |        |          |         |
|      |      |             |        |          |         |
|      |      |             |        |          |         |
|      |      |             |        |          |         |
|      |      |             |        |          |         |
|      |      |             |        |          |         |
|      |      |             |        |          |         |
|      |      |             |        |          |         |
|      |      |             |        |          |         |
|      |      |             |        |          |         |
|      |      |             |        |          |         |
|      |      |             |        |          |         |
|      |      |             |        |          |         |
|      |      |             |        |          |         |
|      |      |             |        |          |         |
|      |      |             |        |          |         |
|      |      |             |        |          |         |
|      |      |             |        |          |         |
|      |      |             |        |          |         |
|      |      | **Total**   |        |          |         |

**NOTE**

# INCOME & EXPENSE
## LOG BOOK

Year:

Month:

| Sr # | Date | Description | Income | Expenses | Balance |
|------|------|-------------|--------|----------|---------|
| | | | | | |
| | | | | | |
| | | | | | |
| | | | | | |
| | | | | | |
| | | | | | |
| | | | | | |
| | | | | | |
| | | | | | |
| | | | | | |
| | | | | | |
| | | | | | |
| | | | | | |
| | | | | | |
| | | | | | |
| | | | | | |
| | | | | | |
| | | | | | |
| | | | | | |
| | | | | | |
| | Total | | | | |

**NOTE**

# INCOME & EXPENSE
## LOG BOOK

**Year:**

**Month:**

| Sr # | Date | Description | Income | Expenses | Balance |
|---|---|---|---|---|---|
| | | | | | |
| | | | | | |
| | | | | | |
| | | | | | |
| | | | | | |
| | | | | | |
| | | | | | |
| | | | | | |
| | | | | | |
| | | | | | |
| | | | | | |
| | | | | | |
| | | | | | |
| | | | | | |
| | | | | | |
| | | | | | |
| | | | | | |
| | | | | | |
| | | | | | |
| | | | | | |
| | | | | | |
| | **Total** | | | | |

**NOTE**

# INCOME & EXPENSE
## LOG BOOK

Year:

Month:

| Sr # | Date | Description | Income | Expenses | Balance |
|------|------|-------------|--------|----------|---------|
| | | | | | |
| | | | | | |
| | | | | | |
| | | | | | |
| | | | | | |
| | | | | | |
| | | | | | |
| | | | | | |
| | | | | | |
| | | | | | |
| | | | | | |
| | | | | | |
| | | | | | |
| | | | | | |
| | | | | | |
| | | | | | |
| | | | | | |
| | | | | | |
| | | | | | |
| | | Total | | | |

**NOTE**

# INCOME & EXPENSE
## LOG BOOK

**Year:**

**Month:**

| Sr # | Date | Description | Income | Expenses | Balance |
|------|------|-------------|--------|----------|---------|
| | | | | | |
| | | | | | |
| | | | | | |
| | | | | | |
| | | | | | |
| | | | | | |
| | | | | | |
| | | | | | |
| | | | | | |
| | | | | | |
| | | | | | |
| | | | | | |
| | | | | | |
| | | | | | |
| | | | | | |
| | | | | | |
| | | | | | |
| | | | | | |
| | | | | | |
| | | Total | | | |

**NOTE**

# INCOME & EXPENSE
## LOG BOOK

Year:

Month:

| Sr # | Date | Description | Income | Expenses | Balance |
|------|------|-------------|--------|----------|---------|
|  |  |  |  |  |  |
|  |  |  |  |  |  |
|  |  |  |  |  |  |
|  |  |  |  |  |  |
|  |  |  |  |  |  |
|  |  |  |  |  |  |
|  |  |  |  |  |  |
|  |  |  |  |  |  |
|  |  |  |  |  |  |
|  |  |  |  |  |  |
|  |  |  |  |  |  |
|  |  |  |  |  |  |
|  |  |  |  |  |  |
|  |  |  |  |  |  |
|  |  |  |  |  |  |
|  |  |  |  |  |  |
|  |  |  |  |  |  |
|  |  |  |  |  |  |
|  |  |  |  |  |  |
|  |  |  |  |  |  |
|  |  | **Total** |  |  |  |

**NOTE**

# INCOME & EXPENSE
## LOG BOOK

**Year:**

**Month:**

| Sr # | Date | Description | Income | Expenses | Balance |
|------|------|-------------|--------|----------|---------|
| | | | | | |
| | | | | | |
| | | | | | |
| | | | | | |
| | | | | | |
| | | | | | |
| | | | | | |
| | | | | | |
| | | | | | |
| | | | | | |
| | | | | | |
| | | | | | |
| | | | | | |
| | | | | | |
| | | | | | |
| | | | | | |
| | | | | | |
| | | | | | |
| | | | | | |
| | | | | | |
| | **Total** | | | | |

**NOTE**

# INCOME & EXPENSE
## LOG BOOK

**Year:**

**Month:**

| Sr # | Date | Description | Income | Expenses | Balance |
|------|------|-------------|--------|----------|---------|
|  |  |  |  |  |  |
|  |  |  |  |  |  |
|  |  |  |  |  |  |
|  |  |  |  |  |  |
|  |  |  |  |  |  |
|  |  |  |  |  |  |
|  |  |  |  |  |  |
|  |  |  |  |  |  |
|  |  |  |  |  |  |
|  |  |  |  |  |  |
|  |  |  |  |  |  |
|  |  |  |  |  |  |
|  |  |  |  |  |  |
|  |  |  |  |  |  |
|  |  |  |  |  |  |
|  |  |  |  |  |  |
|  |  |  |  |  |  |
|  |  |  |  |  |  |
|  |  |  |  |  |  |
|  |  | **Total** |  |  |  |

**NOTE**

# INCOME & EXPENSE
## LOG BOOK

**Year:**

**Month:**

| Sr # | Date | Description | Income | Expenses | Balance |
|---|---|---|---|---|---|
| | | | | | |
| | | | | | |
| | | | | | |
| | | | | | |
| | | | | | |
| | | | | | |
| | | | | | |
| | | | | | |
| | | | | | |
| | | | | | |
| | | | | | |
| | | | | | |
| | | | | | |
| | | | | | |
| | | | | | |
| | | | | | |
| | | | | | |
| | | | | | |
| | | | | | |
| | | | | | |
| | | | | | |
| | **Total** | | | | |

**NOTE**

# INCOME & EXPENSE
## LOG BOOK

**Year:**

**Month:**

| Sr # | Date | Description | Income | Expenses | Balance |
|---|---|---|---|---|---|
| | | | | | |
| | | | | | |
| | | | | | |
| | | | | | |
| | | | | | |
| | | | | | |
| | | | | | |
| | | | | | |
| | | | | | |
| | | | | | |
| | | | | | |
| | | | | | |
| | | | | | |
| | | | | | |
| | | | | | |
| | | | | | |
| | | | | | |
| | | | | | |
| | | | | | |
| | | | | | |
| | | **Total** | | | |

**NOTE**

# INCOME & EXPENSE
## LOG BOOK

**Year:**

**Month:**

| Sr # | Date | Description | Income | Expenses | Balance |
|------|------|-------------|--------|----------|---------|
| | | | | | |
| | | | | | |
| | | | | | |
| | | | | | |
| | | | | | |
| | | | | | |
| | | | | | |
| | | | | | |
| | | | | | |
| | | | | | |
| | | | | | |
| | | | | | |
| | | | | | |
| | | | | | |
| | | | | | |
| | | | | | |
| | | | | | |
| | | | | | |
| | | | | | |
| | | | | | |
| | | | | | |
| | **Total** | | | | |

**NOTE**

# INCOME & EXPENSE
## LOG BOOK

**Year:**

**Month:**

| Sr # | Date | Description | Income | Expenses | Balance |
|---|---|---|---|---|---|
| | | | | | |
| | | | | | |
| | | | | | |
| | | | | | |
| | | | | | |
| | | | | | |
| | | | | | |
| | | | | | |
| | | | | | |
| | | | | | |
| | | | | | |
| | | | | | |
| | | | | | |
| | | | | | |
| | | | | | |
| | | | | | |
| | | | | | |
| | | | | | |
| | | | | | |
| | **Total** | | | | |

**NOTE**

# INCOME & EXPENSE
## LOG BOOK

Year:

Month:

| Sr # | Date | Description | Income | Expenses | Balance |
|------|------|-------------|--------|----------|---------|
| | | | | | |
| | | | | | |
| | | | | | |
| | | | | | |
| | | | | | |
| | | | | | |
| | | | | | |
| | | | | | |
| | | | | | |
| | | | | | |
| | | | | | |
| | | | | | |
| | | | | | |
| | | | | | |
| | | | | | |
| | | | | | |
| | | | | | |
| | | | | | |
| | | | | | |
| | | | | | |
| | | | | | |
| | | | | | |
| | **Total** | | | | |

**NOTE**

# INCOME & EXPENSE
## LOG BOOK

Year: 

Month: 

| Sr # | Date | Description | Income | Expenses | Balance |
|------|------|-------------|--------|----------|---------|
|  |  |  |  |  |  |
|  |  |  |  |  |  |
|  |  |  |  |  |  |
|  |  |  |  |  |  |
|  |  |  |  |  |  |
|  |  |  |  |  |  |
|  |  |  |  |  |  |
|  |  |  |  |  |  |
|  |  |  |  |  |  |
|  |  |  |  |  |  |
|  |  |  |  |  |  |
|  |  |  |  |  |  |
|  |  |  |  |  |  |
|  |  |  |  |  |  |
|  |  |  |  |  |  |
|  |  |  |  |  |  |
|  |  |  |  |  |  |
|  |  |  |  |  |  |
|  |  |  |  |  |  |
|  |  |  |  |  |  |
|  | | **Total** |  |  |  |

**NOTE**

# INCOME & EXPENSE
## LOG BOOK

Year: 

Month: 

| Sr # | Date | Description | Income | Expenses | Balance |
|------|------|-------------|--------|----------|---------|
|      |      |             |        |          |         |
|      |      |             |        |          |         |
|      |      |             |        |          |         |
|      |      |             |        |          |         |
|      |      |             |        |          |         |
|      |      |             |        |          |         |
|      |      |             |        |          |         |
|      |      |             |        |          |         |
|      |      |             |        |          |         |
|      |      |             |        |          |         |
|      |      |             |        |          |         |
|      |      |             |        |          |         |
|      |      |             |        |          |         |
|      |      |             |        |          |         |
|      |      |             |        |          |         |
|      |      |             |        |          |         |
|      |      |             |        |          |         |
|      |      |             |        |          |         |
|      |      |             |        |          |         |
|      |      |             |        |          |         |
|      |      |             |        |          |         |
|      |      | **Total**   |        |          |         |

**NOTE**

# INCOME & EXPENSE
## LOG BOOK

Year: _____

Month: _____

| Sr # | Date | Description | Income | Expenses | Balance |
|------|------|-------------|--------|----------|---------|
| | | | | | |
| | | | | | |
| | | | | | |
| | | | | | |
| | | | | | |
| | | | | | |
| | | | | | |
| | | | | | |
| | | | | | |
| | | | | | |
| | | | | | |
| | | | | | |
| | | | | | |
| | | | | | |
| | | | | | |
| | | | | | |
| | | | | | |
| | | | | | |
| | | | | | |
| | | | | | |
| | | | | | |
| | | | | | |
| | | **Total** | | | |

**NOTE** _____

# INCOME & EXPENSE
## LOG BOOK

Year:

Month:

| Sr # | Date | Description | Income | Expenses | Balance |
|------|------|-------------|--------|----------|---------|
|      |      |             |        |          |         |
|      |      |             |        |          |         |
|      |      |             |        |          |         |
|      |      |             |        |          |         |
|      |      |             |        |          |         |
|      |      |             |        |          |         |
|      |      |             |        |          |         |
|      |      |             |        |          |         |
|      |      |             |        |          |         |
|      |      |             |        |          |         |
|      |      |             |        |          |         |
|      |      |             |        |          |         |
|      |      |             |        |          |         |
|      |      |             |        |          |         |
|      |      |             |        |          |         |
|      |      |             |        |          |         |
|      |      |             |        |          |         |
|      |      |             |        |          |         |
|      |      |             |        |          |         |
|      |      |             |        |          |         |
|      |      |             |        |          |         |
|      |      |             |        |          |         |
|      | **Total** |        |        |          |         |

**NOTE**

# INCOME & EXPENSE
## LOG BOOK

**Year:**

**Month:**

| Sr # | Date | Description | Income | Expenses | Balance |
|---|---|---|---|---|---|
|  |  |  |  |  |  |
|  |  |  |  |  |  |
|  |  |  |  |  |  |
|  |  |  |  |  |  |
|  |  |  |  |  |  |
|  |  |  |  |  |  |
|  |  |  |  |  |  |
|  |  |  |  |  |  |
|  |  |  |  |  |  |
|  |  |  |  |  |  |
|  |  |  |  |  |  |
|  |  |  |  |  |  |
|  |  |  |  |  |  |
|  |  |  |  |  |  |
|  |  |  |  |  |  |
|  |  |  |  |  |  |
|  |  |  |  |  |  |
|  |  |  |  |  |  |
|  |  |  |  |  |  |
|  |  |  |  |  |  |
|  |  | **Total** |  |  |  |

**NOTE**

# INCOME & EXPENSE
## LOG BOOK

Year:

Month:

| Sr # | Date | Description | Income | Expenses | Balance |
|------|------|-------------|--------|----------|---------|
|  |  |  |  |  |  |
|  |  |  |  |  |  |
|  |  |  |  |  |  |
|  |  |  |  |  |  |
|  |  |  |  |  |  |
|  |  |  |  |  |  |
|  |  |  |  |  |  |
|  |  |  |  |  |  |
|  |  |  |  |  |  |
|  |  |  |  |  |  |
|  |  |  |  |  |  |
|  |  |  |  |  |  |
|  |  |  |  |  |  |
|  |  |  |  |  |  |
|  |  |  |  |  |  |
|  |  |  |  |  |  |
|  |  |  |  |  |  |
|  |  |  |  |  |  |
|  |  |  |  |  |  |
|  |  |  |  |  |  |
|  |  |  |  |  |  |
|  | | **Total** |  |  |  |

**NOTE**

# INCOME & EXPENSE
## LOG BOOK

Year:

Month:

| Sr # | Date | Description | Income | Expenses | Balance |
|---|---|---|---|---|---|
| | | | | | |
| | | | | | |
| | | | | | |
| | | | | | |
| | | | | | |
| | | | | | |
| | | | | | |
| | | | | | |
| | | | | | |
| | | | | | |
| | | | | | |
| | | | | | |
| | | | | | |
| | | | | | |
| | | | | | |
| | | | | | |
| | | | | | |
| | | | | | |
| | | | | | |
| | | | | | |
| | | Total | | | |

**NOTE**

# INCOME & EXPENSE
## LOG BOOK

Year: 

Month: 

| Sr # | Date | Description | Income | Expenses | Balance |
|---|---|---|---|---|---|
| | | | | | |
| | | | | | |
| | | | | | |
| | | | | | |
| | | | | | |
| | | | | | |
| | | | | | |
| | | | | | |
| | | | | | |
| | | | | | |
| | | | | | |
| | | | | | |
| | | | | | |
| | | | | | |
| | | | | | |
| | | | | | |
| | | | | | |
| | | | | | |
| | | | | | |
| | | | | | |
| | | | | | |
| | | | | | |
| | | Total | | | |

**NOTE**

# INCOME & EXPENSE
## LOG BOOK

Year:

Month:

| Sr # | Date | Description | Income | Expenses | Balance |
|------|------|-------------|--------|----------|---------|
| | | | | | |
| | | | | | |
| | | | | | |
| | | | | | |
| | | | | | |
| | | | | | |
| | | | | | |
| | | | | | |
| | | | | | |
| | | | | | |
| | | | | | |
| | | | | | |
| | | | | | |
| | | | | | |
| | | | | | |
| | | | | | |
| | | | | | |
| | | | | | |
| | | | | | |
| | | | | | |
| | | | | | |
| | | **Total** | | | |

**NOTE**

# INCOME & EXPENSE
## LOG BOOK

**Year:**

**Month:**

| Sr # | Date | Description | Income | Expenses | Balance |
|------|------|-------------|--------|----------|---------|
|      |      |             |        |          |         |
|      |      |             |        |          |         |
|      |      |             |        |          |         |
|      |      |             |        |          |         |
|      |      |             |        |          |         |
|      |      |             |        |          |         |
|      |      |             |        |          |         |
|      |      |             |        |          |         |
|      |      |             |        |          |         |
|      |      |             |        |          |         |
|      |      |             |        |          |         |
|      |      |             |        |          |         |
|      |      |             |        |          |         |
|      |      |             |        |          |         |
|      |      |             |        |          |         |
|      |      |             |        |          |         |
|      |      |             |        |          |         |
|      |      |             |        |          |         |
|      |      |             |        |          |         |
|      |      |             |        |          |         |
|      |      |             |        |          |         |
|      |      |             |        |          |         |
|      |      |             |        |          |         |
|      |      | **Total**   |        |          |         |

**NOTE**

# INCOME & EXPENSE
## LOG BOOK

Year: 

Month: 

| Sr # | Date | Description | Income | Expenses | Balance |
|------|------|-------------|--------|----------|---------|
|      |      |             |        |          |         |
|      |      |             |        |          |         |
|      |      |             |        |          |         |
|      |      |             |        |          |         |
|      |      |             |        |          |         |
|      |      |             |        |          |         |
|      |      |             |        |          |         |
|      |      |             |        |          |         |
|      |      |             |        |          |         |
|      |      |             |        |          |         |
|      |      |             |        |          |         |
|      |      |             |        |          |         |
|      |      |             |        |          |         |
|      |      |             |        |          |         |
|      |      |             |        |          |         |
|      |      |             |        |          |         |
|      |      |             |        |          |         |
|      |      |             |        |          |         |
|      |      |             |        |          |         |
|      |      |             |        |          |         |
|      |      |             |        |          |         |
|      | **Total** |        |        |          |         |

**NOTE**

# INCOME & EXPENSE
## LOG BOOK

Year: 

Month: 

| Sr # | Date | Description | Income | Expenses | Balance |
|------|------|-------------|--------|----------|---------|
| | | | | | |
| | | | | | |
| | | | | | |
| | | | | | |
| | | | | | |
| | | | | | |
| | | | | | |
| | | | | | |
| | | | | | |
| | | | | | |
| | | | | | |
| | | | | | |
| | | | | | |
| | | | | | |
| | | | | | |
| | | | | | |
| | | | | | |
| | | | | | |
| | | | | | |
| | | | | | |
| | | | | | |
| | | | | | |
| | | | | | |
| | | Total | | | |

**NOTE**

# INCOME & EXPENSE
## LOG BOOK

**Year:**

**Month:**

| Sr # | Date | Description | Income | Expenses | Balance |
|------|------|-------------|--------|----------|---------|
|      |      |             |        |          |         |
|      |      |             |        |          |         |
|      |      |             |        |          |         |
|      |      |             |        |          |         |
|      |      |             |        |          |         |
|      |      |             |        |          |         |
|      |      |             |        |          |         |
|      |      |             |        |          |         |
|      |      |             |        |          |         |
|      |      |             |        |          |         |
|      |      |             |        |          |         |
|      |      |             |        |          |         |
|      |      |             |        |          |         |
|      |      |             |        |          |         |
|      |      |             |        |          |         |
|      |      |             |        |          |         |
|      |      |             |        |          |         |
|      |      |             |        |          |         |
|      |      |             |        |          |         |
|      |      |             |        |          |         |
|      |      | **Total**   |        |          |         |

**NOTE**

# INCOME & EXPENSE
## LOG BOOK

Year:

Month:

| Sr # | Date | Description | Income | Expenses | Balance |
|------|------|-------------|--------|----------|---------|
| | | | | | |
| | | | | | |
| | | | | | |
| | | | | | |
| | | | | | |
| | | | | | |
| | | | | | |
| | | | | | |
| | | | | | |
| | | | | | |
| | | | | | |
| | | | | | |
| | | | | | |
| | | | | | |
| | | | | | |
| | | | | | |
| | | | | | |
| | | | | | |
| | | | | | |
| | | | | | |
| | | | | | |
| | | | | | |
| | | Total | | | |

**NOTE**

# INCOME & EXPENSE
## LOG BOOK

Year:

Month:

| Sr # | Date | Description | Income | Expenses | Balance |
|------|------|-------------|--------|----------|---------|
|  |  |  |  |  |  |
|  |  |  |  |  |  |
|  |  |  |  |  |  |
|  |  |  |  |  |  |
|  |  |  |  |  |  |
|  |  |  |  |  |  |
|  |  |  |  |  |  |
|  |  |  |  |  |  |
|  |  |  |  |  |  |
|  |  |  |  |  |  |
|  |  |  |  |  |  |
|  |  |  |  |  |  |
|  |  |  |  |  |  |
|  |  |  |  |  |  |
|  |  |  |  |  |  |
|  |  |  |  |  |  |
|  |  |  |  |  |  |
|  |  |  |  |  |  |
|  |  |  |  |  |  |
|  |  | **Total** |  |  |  |

**NOTE**

# INCOME & EXPENSE
## LOG BOOK

Year:

Month:

| Sr # | Date | Description | Income | Expenses | Balance |
|------|------|-------------|--------|----------|---------|
|      |      |             |        |          |         |
|      |      |             |        |          |         |
|      |      |             |        |          |         |
|      |      |             |        |          |         |
|      |      |             |        |          |         |
|      |      |             |        |          |         |
|      |      |             |        |          |         |
|      |      |             |        |          |         |
|      |      |             |        |          |         |
|      |      |             |        |          |         |
|      |      |             |        |          |         |
|      |      |             |        |          |         |
|      |      |             |        |          |         |
|      |      |             |        |          |         |
|      |      |             |        |          |         |
|      |      |             |        |          |         |
|      |      |             |        |          |         |
|      |      |             |        |          |         |
|      |      |             |        |          |         |
|      |      |             |        |          |         |
|      |      | **Total**   |        |          |         |

**NOTE**

# INCOME & EXPENSE
## LOG BOOK

Year:

Month:

| Sr # | Date | Description | Income | Expenses | Balance |
|------|------|-------------|--------|----------|---------|
| | | | | | |
| | | | | | |
| | | | | | |
| | | | | | |
| | | | | | |
| | | | | | |
| | | | | | |
| | | | | | |
| | | | | | |
| | | | | | |
| | | | | | |
| | | | | | |
| | | | | | |
| | | | | | |
| | | | | | |
| | | | | | |
| | | | | | |
| | | | | | |
| | | | | | |
| | | | | | |
| | | Total | | | |

**NOTE**

# INCOME & EXPENSE
## LOG BOOK

Year:

Month:

| Sr # | Date | Description | Income | Expenses | Balance |
|------|------|-------------|--------|----------|---------|
|  |  |  |  |  |  |
|  |  |  |  |  |  |
|  |  |  |  |  |  |
|  |  |  |  |  |  |
|  |  |  |  |  |  |
|  |  |  |  |  |  |
|  |  |  |  |  |  |
|  |  |  |  |  |  |
|  |  |  |  |  |  |
|  |  |  |  |  |  |
|  |  |  |  |  |  |
|  |  |  |  |  |  |
|  |  |  |  |  |  |
|  |  |  |  |  |  |
|  |  |  |  |  |  |
|  |  |  |  |  |  |
|  |  |  |  |  |  |
|  |  |  |  |  |  |
|  |  |  |  |  |  |
|  |  |  |  |  |  |
|  |  |  |  |  |  |
|  |  |  |  |  |  |
|  |  | **Total** |  |  |  |

**NOTE**

# INCOME & EXPENSE
## LOG BOOK

Year: 
Month: 

| Sr # | Date | Description | Income | Expenses | Balance |
|------|------|-------------|--------|----------|---------|
|  |  |  |  |  |  |
|  |  |  |  |  |  |
|  |  |  |  |  |  |
|  |  |  |  |  |  |
|  |  |  |  |  |  |
|  |  |  |  |  |  |
|  |  |  |  |  |  |
|  |  |  |  |  |  |
|  |  |  |  |  |  |
|  |  |  |  |  |  |
|  |  |  |  |  |  |
|  |  |  |  |  |  |
|  |  |  |  |  |  |
|  |  |  |  |  |  |
|  |  |  |  |  |  |
|  |  |  |  |  |  |
|  |  |  |  |  |  |
|  |  |  |  |  |  |
|  |  |  |  |  |  |
|  |  |  |  |  |  |
| | | **Total** | | | |

**NOTE**

# INCOME & EXPENSE
## LOG BOOK

Year:

Month:

| Sr # | Date | Description | Income | Expenses | Balance |
|------|------|-------------|--------|----------|---------|
| | | | | | |
| | | | | | |
| | | | | | |
| | | | | | |
| | | | | | |
| | | | | | |
| | | | | | |
| | | | | | |
| | | | | | |
| | | | | | |
| | | | | | |
| | | | | | |
| | | | | | |
| | | | | | |
| | | | | | |
| | | | | | |
| | | | | | |
| | | | | | |
| | | | | | |
| | | | | | |
| | | | | | |
| | | | | | |
| | | | | | |
| | **Total** | | | | |

**NOTE**

# INCOME & EXPENSE
## LOG BOOK

Year: _____

Month: _____

| Sr # | Date | Description | Income | Expenses | Balance |
|------|------|-------------|--------|----------|---------|
|      |      |             |        |          |         |
|      |      |             |        |          |         |
|      |      |             |        |          |         |
|      |      |             |        |          |         |
|      |      |             |        |          |         |
|      |      |             |        |          |         |
|      |      |             |        |          |         |
|      |      |             |        |          |         |
|      |      |             |        |          |         |
|      |      |             |        |          |         |
|      |      |             |        |          |         |
|      |      |             |        |          |         |
|      |      |             |        |          |         |
|      |      |             |        |          |         |
|      |      |             |        |          |         |
|      |      |             |        |          |         |
|      |      |             |        |          |         |
|      |      |             |        |          |         |
|      |      |             |        |          |         |
|      |      |             |        |          |         |
|      |      | **Total**   |        |          |         |

**NOTE**

# INCOME & EXPENSE
## LOG BOOK

**Year:**

**Month:**

| Sr # | Date | Description | Income | Expenses | Balance |
|------|------|-------------|--------|----------|---------|
|  |  |  |  |  |  |
|  |  |  |  |  |  |
|  |  |  |  |  |  |
|  |  |  |  |  |  |
|  |  |  |  |  |  |
|  |  |  |  |  |  |
|  |  |  |  |  |  |
|  |  |  |  |  |  |
|  |  |  |  |  |  |
|  |  |  |  |  |  |
|  |  |  |  |  |  |
|  |  |  |  |  |  |
|  |  |  |  |  |  |
|  |  |  |  |  |  |
|  |  |  |  |  |  |
|  |  |  |  |  |  |
|  |  |  |  |  |  |
|  |  |  |  |  |  |
|  |  |  |  |  |  |
|  |  |  |  |  |  |
|  |  |  |  |  |  |
|  |  |  |  |  |  |
|  |  |  |  |  |  |
|  |  |  |  |  |  |
| | | **Total** |  |  |  |

**NOTE**

# INCOME & EXPENSE
## LOG BOOK

Year:

Month:

| Sr # | Date | Description | Income | Expenses | Balance |
|------|------|-------------|--------|----------|---------|
| | | | | | |
| | | | | | |
| | | | | | |
| | | | | | |
| | | | | | |
| | | | | | |
| | | | | | |
| | | | | | |
| | | | | | |
| | | | | | |
| | | | | | |
| | | | | | |
| | | | | | |
| | | | | | |
| | | | | | |
| | | | | | |
| | | | | | |
| | | | | | |
| | | | | | |
| | | | | | |
| | **Total** | | | | |

**NOTE**

# INCOME & EXPENSE
## LOG BOOK

**Year:**

**Month:**

| Sr # | Date | Description | Income | Expenses | Balance |
|------|------|-------------|--------|----------|---------|
| | | | | | |
| | | | | | |
| | | | | | |
| | | | | | |
| | | | | | |
| | | | | | |
| | | | | | |
| | | | | | |
| | | | | | |
| | | | | | |
| | | | | | |
| | | | | | |
| | | | | | |
| | | | | | |
| | | | | | |
| | | | | | |
| | | | | | |
| | | | | | |
| | | | | | |
| | | | | | |
| | | | | | |
| | | | | | |
| | | | | | |
| | | **Total** | | | |

**NOTE**

# INCOME & EXPENSE
## LOG BOOK

**Year:**

**Month:**

| Sr # | Date | Description | Income | Expenses | Balance |
|------|------|-------------|--------|----------|---------|
|      |      |             |        |          |         |
|      |      |             |        |          |         |
|      |      |             |        |          |         |
|      |      |             |        |          |         |
|      |      |             |        |          |         |
|      |      |             |        |          |         |
|      |      |             |        |          |         |
|      |      |             |        |          |         |
|      |      |             |        |          |         |
|      |      |             |        |          |         |
|      |      |             |        |          |         |
|      |      |             |        |          |         |
|      |      |             |        |          |         |
|      |      |             |        |          |         |
|      |      |             |        |          |         |
|      |      |             |        |          |         |
|      |      |             |        |          |         |
|      |      |             |        |          |         |
|      |      |             |        |          |         |
|      |      |             |        |          |         |
|      | **Total** |        |        |          |         |

**NOTE**

# INCOME & EXPENSE
## LOG BOOK

**Year:**

**Month:**

| Sr # | Date | Description | Income | Expenses | Balance |
|------|------|-------------|--------|----------|---------|
|      |      |             |        |          |         |
|      |      |             |        |          |         |
|      |      |             |        |          |         |
|      |      |             |        |          |         |
|      |      |             |        |          |         |
|      |      |             |        |          |         |
|      |      |             |        |          |         |
|      |      |             |        |          |         |
|      |      |             |        |          |         |
|      |      |             |        |          |         |
|      |      |             |        |          |         |
|      |      |             |        |          |         |
|      |      |             |        |          |         |
|      |      |             |        |          |         |
|      |      |             |        |          |         |
|      |      |             |        |          |         |
|      |      |             |        |          |         |
|      |      |             |        |          |         |
|      |      |             |        |          |         |
|      |      |             |        |          |         |
|      |      |             |        |          |         |
|      |      |             |        |          |         |
|      |      | **Total**   |        |          |         |

**NOTE**

# INCOME & EXPENSE
## LOG BOOK

**Year:**

**Month:**

| Sr # | Date | Description | Income | Expenses | Balance |
|------|------|-------------|--------|----------|---------|
| | | | | | |
| | | | | | |
| | | | | | |
| | | | | | |
| | | | | | |
| | | | | | |
| | | | | | |
| | | | | | |
| | | | | | |
| | | | | | |
| | | | | | |
| | | | | | |
| | | | | | |
| | | | | | |
| | | | | | |
| | | | | | |
| | | | | | |
| | | | | | |
| | | | | | |
| | | | | | |
| | **Total** | | | | |

**NOTE**

# INCOME & EXPENSE
## LOG BOOK

Year:

Month:

| Sr # | Date | Description | Income | Expenses | Balance |
|------|------|-------------|--------|----------|---------|
| | | | | | |
| | | | | | |
| | | | | | |
| | | | | | |
| | | | | | |
| | | | | | |
| | | | | | |
| | | | | | |
| | | | | | |
| | | | | | |
| | | | | | |
| | | | | | |
| | | | | | |
| | | | | | |
| | | | | | |
| | | | | | |
| | | | | | |
| | | | | | |
| | | | | | |
| | | | | | |
| | | Total | | | |

**NOTE**